T0158222

This book is dedicated to my wife and best friend, Papri Das, who inspired me to write poems.

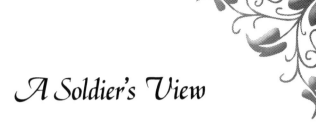

A Soldier's View

I am a soldier born to serve my nation;

I serve my motherland with full dedication.

I don't know what are intolerance and discrimination;

I guard the borders so that you can sleep without any hesitation.

I don't do this in the name of any race, creed, or religion, any
differentiation;

I am only to serve my country with full determination.

I feel proud even to die for my great nation;

Thinking of dying for my country gives me immense satisfaction.

I don't want to be in headlines or in discussions on any primetime
news;

I want my fellow citizens to be broad-minded without any narrow
views.

I may even die tomorrow knowing nobody can take my place in my
family,

But if I don't get ready to die, nobody can ever enjoy his
independence freely.

Bird

Bird can fly anywhere in this world without any restriction;
Bird can move from one place to another without any permission.
Bird is a symbol of peace and freedom;
Bird lives life like a king but has no kingdom.
Bird has no boundary in life for where it needs to fly;
Bird likes to see the whole world in its own way before it must die.
Bird lives in its own world without any obligation;
Bird needs no fame, so it doesn't go for any reconciliation.
Bird can't be kept in a cage even with a high wage;
Bird also can never be controlled even with a rage.
Bird could never live even for a second without its wings;
Only Bird's wings can fulfil all its ultimate dreams.

My Feelings for You

About my feelings for you, I know you don't have any clue,

But my feelings for you are really very true.

My feelings for you are like having something without any
expectation,

But my feelings are strong without any negation.

My feelings for you give my mind such pleasure,

But my feelings have got no bad desire.

My feelings for you really give myself much joy,

And my feelings for you also turn me from a man to a boy.

My feelings for you help me live in my own world of fantasy,

But my feelings for you also turn me away from any other ecstasy.

My feelings for you within me create something which can't be
explained,

And my feelings for you also help negativity within me get
restrained.

God

There is God, and He is one.

Without Him, long back we could have gone.

But still, we on our own divide one God;

In His name, still we break our own harmony chord.

We still fight, taking His different name,

And we only in His name bring humanity into shame.

By taking His name when we are bringing destruction,

We call it nothing but religious revolution.

Oh God, why have You made so many human beings,

As they take Your name to become hobgoblins?

Little Angel

Little angel came into our life;
She gave us new joy and a reason to survive.
Her smile is the reason for all our grief's destruction;
Her small touch gives us immense satisfaction.
Her innocent face has no fabrication;
Her love for us has full dedication.
She has a mind with so much purity,
As if nothing in this world could have that much clarity.
Her every question is so simple yet meaningful,
So sometimes to answer it, we have to become thoughtful.
Little angel is like a newly born small blossom,
But every day, she is teaching us a new lesson.
Little angel, now I am from you quite far away,
But in your heart, I always like to stay.

Freedom

We want freedom and want to become free,
But we live in a cage and are afraid to flee.
We want peace of mind to become free
But we can't leave the cage full of luxury.
In freedom, we always want to be happy,
But for this, we run only after money.
We want freedom so that we can move far away,
But beyond our luxury cage, we can't find a way.
We want freedom so as to live our own way in life,
But we are afraid of leaving our luxury hive.

Solace

I just want to go to a really nice place,

Where I can walk at my own slow pace.

I don't want a place where people only show a false attitude;

I want a place with sanctity and complete solitude.

The only person I want in that place is you,

As you are the only one able to understand my view.

In that place, you can purify my mind with a prod,

Even without uttering to me a single word.

Love is there but, in this world, quite difficult to find,

As people have heart but think only through conscious mind.

I find myself quite unfit in this crowded place,

So I'd like to flee with you somewhere to get true solace.

Feelings of Love

I just want to go missing from this world; please don't let me do so.

I am searching for true love within you, so don't consider me
your foe.

I know you've got yourself attached elsewhere,

But my heart, I have your picture, which I can see everywhere.

I know you may not like my feelings, as for you, they may not be
fair,

But for you, I can do anything which others cannot even dare.

I know I cannot tell you in front of the whole world, "I love you,"

But believe me, my feelings for you in my heart are really very true.

I just want to put myself within you in life at least once

So I am able to experience your love in my own trance.

You are for me nothing less than a diva;

Only through your love I want to get true nirvana.

Need to Change This Changed World

The world where once I was born has changed a lot;

Some people may believe it, and others may not.

In the world today, each and every day just to survive, we need to fight;

While fighting, we are forgetting what is wrong and what is right.

Peaceful religions are being changed into fanaticism.

People are becoming more restless, and one can hardly see any humanism.

Everyone seems to run after a mirage of money to win his own race

But forget that a mirage can never give him true solace.

People prefer to meet each other through social networks rather than face to face,

And to prove oneself superior, one doesn't mind to put others in disgrace.

Honesty today is on the verge of extinction

As wealth becomes the only yardstick to determine one's reputation.

We need to change this changed world once again;

Otherwise, opulence will put mankind in a prison with a chain.

Different Love

Who is saying that love needs a name?
Love needs feelings only, without any fame.
I know you love me and I love you,
But it's difficult for others to understand our view.
Love doesn't mean that you need to marry;
Love means true feelings need to carry.
Feelings are there and will be there
For which you don't need others to fear.
If my kiss on your lips can give you joy,
Then you have got every right to enjoy.
I want you in front of me to be nude
So I can make love with you without being rude.
Life is one, so please don't hesitate;
Otherwise, your life will become a complete waste.
I know you deserve to get all your pleasures;
I want to fulfil all your feelings and inner desires.

By Looking into Your Eyes

By looking into your eyes, I can see how much you love me.

By looking into your eyes, I can see the prison from which you want to break free.

By looking into your eyes, I can see a world full of simplicity.

By looking into your eyes, I always try to find within you my own destiny.

By looking into your eyes, I can see your mind, where there is no vanity.

By looking into your eyes, only I can feel within my heart a true form of amity.

By looking into your eyes, I can get the power to fight for you against this hypocritical society.

By looking into your eyes, I only can find myself in a world full of liberty.

By looking into your eyes, I find myself in a world full of illusionary illustration.

By looking into your eyes, I can overcome any type of frustration.

By looking into your eyes, I am getting true courage with strong determination.

By looking into your eyes, I just want to get a true form of salvation.

A Smile

A smile can change a world in its own way;
A smile can give joy to many without any pay.
A smile can stop a quarrel before it can happen;
A smile can easily stop true love from getting it dampen.
A smile can conquer the hearts of millions without any force;
A smile can give confidence among the defeated as a new source.
A smile can give hope to losers to become winners again;
A smile can help one easily in life cross a rough terrain.
A smile can turn a complicated world into a simple one;
A smile can also bring someone heroism even if he has none.
A smile can convey so many things without the need of a single word;
A smile can give oneself the power of freedom to fly like a free bird.

A Small Girl's View

I am a five-year-old girl;
Each of my eyes is like a pearl.
I like to play here and there,
Without any scold or fear.
I just sometimes like to study
And sometimes like to be a bit naughty.
I just like to breathe fresh air
And don't want pollution anywhere.
I want the whole world, like me, to be simple,
But still, everyone should have a strong principle.
I want a peaceful world without a fight
And like to see everybody holding each other's hands tight.
I want for me no discrimination
So I can grow up freely with strong determination.

Alone

Today, I am feeling in this world so alone,

As the minds of the people around me have not grown.

It's really very difficult for me to understand

Why people like to create a false image and name it a brand.

People think only by showing off they can get anything,

And for them, values and ethics have no meaning.

To get happiness, everyone is running after a false illusion

But isn't able to find for it any solution.

Honesty today has no place for it to go,

And corruption is everywhere, putting on its own show.

People now think they can get everything with money,

Forgetting that after death, no one can take with him a single penny.

Today, my thoughts may seem to many people quite baseless,

But I like to live alone, rather than become spineless.

Living Alone

Living alone helps one become strong against all worldly might;

Living alone gives one the power against all the evils to fight.

Living alone helps one live his life with his own attitude;

Living alone helps one enjoy his life in his own solitude.

Living alone helps one abandon his dependence on any other;

Living alone helps one move ahead in life a bit further.

Living alone helps one understand his true friend and his true enemy;

Living alone helps one live life without needing anyone's sympathy.

Living alone helps one make decisions in life without anybody's intervention;

Living alone gives one the right to live life with so much variation.

Living alone gives one the confidence to live his life in his own way;

But living alone also drifts one from his near and dear ones, quite far away.

Inspiration

Each of your words is giving me inspiration;

Your words are helping my life find a new direction.

My life was full of confusion and dissatisfaction,

But now your kind words are helping me fight them with strong
determination.

Today, I know for me there is someone

Who is a bit different and is not selfish like everyone.

I know you are from me quite far away,

But I still think my life is under your sway.

I don't know whether my expressions are giving you any sense,

But at present, my life is only under your influence.

Today in my life, if I do anything wrong out of a grudge,

I only want you to be there to judge.

My life beforehand never seemed to be so nice,

But today under your inspiration, it is like living in paradise.

True Love

I have some feelings for you;

It may sound awkward, but it's true.

I know it's not possible for you to understand,

But I always feel like sitting beside you, touching your hand.

My true feelings for you will always be here,

So I like to express them to you without any fear.

I know it's never possible for you to come to me,

So in dreams, with you I always like to flee.

I love you for your simplicity and maturity,

A rare combination never found in my mind's vicinity.

Your picture I always keep in my mind,

As I found true love within you of a different kind.

I know we can never be together,

But my love for you will stay forever.

Intolerance

Intolerance is now a hot topic for a lot of discussions;

Intolerance is something which divides a nation into two sections.

Intolerance for some is just a mixture of all political gimmicks;

Intolerance for others is a hidden agenda of some freaks.

Intolerance for some is a conspiracy to take the nation backward;

Intolerance for others is the killing of innocents like a coward.

Intolerance is not a new issue in a country like India;

Intolerance is also not a debate to be shouted in the media.

Intolerance is something which needs to be studied in depth;

Intolerance should also be separated from someone's own faith.

Intolerance is something which needs to be there in democracy;

Intolerance is expected to eradicate the curse of poverty.

Intolerance is an obligation to fight against the evil of corruption;

Intolerance is required to uproot those who don't believe in our
    Constitution.

Intolerance is needed so that no woman in this country is raped;

Intolerance is demanded if a society is improperly shaped.

Intolerance is necessary against those who try to stop freedom of
    speech;

Intolerance is needed to stop a proper system from getting a glitch.

Nirbhaya

She was a simple girl with so many dreams,

But she lay on the road, and nobody heard her screams.

When those demons shattered her, plucking out all her feathers,

We only protested by walking with candles in hand together.

We are for her in the media still fighting and shouting,

But demons in the street are freely dancing.

We think we are in a country which is so civilized,

But women in our society are still quite marginalized.

Today as a doctor, she could have saved so many lives,

But because of our indifference, she didn't get a chance to survive.

One demon is still roaming freely without any shame,

And one honest leader is rehabilitating him for votes and fame.

Even some lawyers are still after her to refute

So they are easily able to save a mindless brute.

If we all need justice for her to become fair,

Bring a law so that no demon by force dares a woman to bare.

Rich Man and Ordinary Man

Rich Man is riding in a Mercedes, and Ordinary Man is just walking down a street.

Rich Man can never accept defeat, and Ordinary Man always needs to retreat.

Rich Man is the exclusive member of a club controlling almost all a country's wealth.

Ordinary Man earns little income and neglects his own health.

Rich Man is a guy who can control the system because of his great money.

Ordinary Man is forced to wear sometimes-torn shoes or clothes and looks so silly.

Rich Man is a guy who doesn't bother to vote but still can control a government.

Ordinary Man is a guy who elects a minister who never gets his appointment.

Rich Man can evade taxes and can easily move away from the country.

Ordinary Man always needs to pay taxes even with great difficulty.

Rich Man needs Ordinary Man so that he can live life with his own illusion.

Ordinary Man can show Rich Man his real place by bringing a country into a new revolution.

Complicated Life

Life is so complicated I don't know where to go;

Life is so complicated that my feelings I am not able to show.

Life is so complicated that I can't break myself free;

Life is so complicated that I am not from distress able to flee.

Life is so complicated that I need to burn myself with a flame;

Life is so complicated that I need to show off to have fame.

Life is so complicated that I can't be in this world the way I am;

Life is so complicated that to stop emotions, I have to build around my mind a self-centered dam.

Life is so complicated that I am not able to enjoy everywhere freedom of speech;

Life is so complicated that of good things I find it quite hard to preach.

Life is so complicated that true love I am not easily able to find;

Life is so complicated that for success, I have to become selfish of a different kind.

Life is so complicated that I am not freely able to enjoy my own life;

Life is so complicated that I need to destroy others to thrive.

Life is so complicated that I need to stay with someone without even finding with her any bond;

Life is so complicated that even after loving someone truly, I am not able to move with her a little beyond.

Getting Lost to Run Away

I am getting lost somewhere in this world among a big crowd,
As I want to live life on my own terms to always feel proud.
I don't want anyone to dictate to me what to do and what to not;
I want to be a free bird and don't want anyone to tie me with a knot.
I have only one life which in my own way I want to set
So that in the future I should in no way have any regret.
I want to enjoy life always and don't want to feel in any way sad,
For which I don't care whether others are feeling good or bad.
I have only one life, so why should I confine myself in a cage
And out of frustration whip others to discharge my own rage?
I want to remain original and cannot change myself for others' sake;
I also don't know how to act just like a fake.
But the people around me always want me to follow their way;
I don't want to be like them, so from them, I prefer to run away.

The Prostitute

The woman is standing on the corner of a quite busy street;
Some people are looking at her with hatred and many with greed.
She has forgotten today to see her own nice dream
But still needs to keep on her face a silly grin.
Civil society has completely driven her out,
So she needs to satisfy civil men without being able to shout.
Nobody is there to understand how for herself she should feel,
So all her inner pain in her heart she has to conceal.
No man wants his mother, daughter, or sister to be like her,
But still only a man is going to her with a loose character.
If, after having her, a man can still live with honour,
Is it right for us to treat her with dishonour?
Rather than pushing her out, we must help her rehabilitate
So that she can also live in this world with some respect.

Falling in Love

Falling in love is not just a normal feeling;

Falling in love is like from a severe pain getting quick healing.

Falling in love gives one's heart real joy;

Falling in love sometimes turns a mature man into a simple boy.

Falling in love cannot always be defined by logic;

Falling in love may change your life, a lot like magic.

Falling in love can make oneself feel sometimes in a maze;

Falling in love has the power to turn a criminal into a sage.

Falling in love can bring the world around someone to a standstill;

Falling in love means in one's heart, true love one needs to feel.

Falling in love doesn't mean the person you love in the same way
    will reciprocate;

Falling in love means to give the person whom you love true respect.

Happiness

Happiness is a feeling which is quite hard to explain;

Happiness is a dream which relieves us from all pain.

Happiness is something which gives true joy to our heart;

Happiness is something which can never be brought by any means to this earth.

Happiness for some may be to love someone without any condition;

Happiness for others may be to fight for a cause with strong determination.

Happiness may be for one to live in solitude and explore his own lost gloss;

Happiness may be for another is helping others without thinking of his own loss.

Happiness for some may be spending time with friends without any reason;

Happiness for others may be getting freedom rather than living in his own prison.

Happiness for me is to see a world in peace without any war;

Happiness for me also is to see everyone from inequality and poverty living quite far.

Beyond the Sky

Beyond the sky, I want to go and fly;

Beyond the sky, I want to go after saying to everyone out here, "Goodbye."

Beyond the sky, I want to build a world of my own;

Beyond the sky, in my world, everyone will be happy without any mourn.

Beyond the sky, there will be a single world without any nation;

Beyond the sky, there will be a world without any discrimination.

Beyond the sky, in that world, there will be God without any religion with a symbol or portrait;

Beyond the sky, in that world, one can find only love without for anyone any hatred.

Beyond the sky, in that world, there will be equal opportunity for everyone to grow;

Beyond the sky, in that world, one can find only friends and not a single foe.

Beyond the sky, in that world, there will be only peace and no war;

Beyond the sky, in that world, greed and selfishness will remain from it quite far.

The Lovely Lady

The lovely lady has got such elegance

That I always feel delighted in her presence.

She has a face full of innocence

But always wants to keep herself within a fence.

She always smiles as if nothing she needs to gain,

So within her lovely smile, she keeps all her pain.

She is working hard, sacrificing everything and has no time to complain,

But still keeps a smiling face; how, nobody can explain.

Lovely lady, I don't want you to slay your happiness;

I just want you to drain from you all your sadness.

Lovely lady, I just want you always to be my benefactress

So I can never find myself in my life in any stress.

Love

Love doesn't mean just staying together;

Love means feeling the same way for each other.

Love means a passion in the heart which can't be explained;

Love means a purity and sanctity which can never be feigned

Love means true feelings without any ploy;

Love means divinity within the heart to enjoy.

Love means a philosophy with no give-and-take;

Love means true belief without being a fake.

Love means something more than faith;

Love means living for each other even after death.

Love means even in absence feeling one's presence;

Love means thinking with a true essence.

Love is something which can go beyond this earth;

Love means a treasure which can never get dearth.

Woman

She is running from morning till evening without any rest

So that everyone remains happy in her own small nest.

She is doing all her work with so much dedication,

But nobody thinks of paying her a little veneration.

She has to do everything without expecting anything in return,

And for others' faults, she also needs to take the burn.

She keeps a life within her for nine months without a time to
    complain,

And for everybody's happiness, she also needs to bear the pain.

She always keeps for others a smiling face

And never gets time to think of her distress.

When she gives a man all forms of pleasure,

Then why does she need to live her life in despair?

Without a woman, mankind has no existence,

But still before her birth, she gets a death sentence.

Many people think a woman nothing more than a commodity;

This means nothing but shame for all of humanity.

Today, to move the world really forward,

Every woman should be given her due regard.

Heart and Brain

My heart is telling me to love you without any condition;

My brain is protesting, as it may lead to total destruction.

My heart is telling me that my feelings for you are true;

My brain is telling me I've got an illusion in the form of you.

My heart is telling me to tell the whole world that without you, I cannot live;

My brain is telling me not to do so, as it may lead to a problem from which I may never get a reprieve.

My heart is telling me you are my true love, as within you, I get complete peace;

My brain is telling me that you are nothing but my mind's disease.

My heart is telling me that I should be with you, as within you, there is not a single dearth;

My brain is telling me I cannot live with you due to so-called customs of this earth.

I know I have nothing to do other than follow my brain,

And I need to keep you within my heart with a pain.

I Love You

I love you even knowing that I can never get you.

I love you, and I know about it, you don't have any clue.

I love you, as on you, I can completely rely.

I love you because for my every question, you have a reply.

I love you, as you are a rare diamond to find.

I love you, and my feelings for you nobody is able to grind.

I love you, and my love, no one can ever understand.

I love you, and for it, I don't have to shout like a big brand.

I love you and will not let others about it know.

I love you, and I don't need the whole world for it to show.

I love you because of your courage and strong determination.

I love you, and within you, I can get my salvation.

I love you, for which I don't need anything in return.

I love you and will till my last breath, even if from me you always run.

The Mountain

The mountain is standing tall and high,
But nobody can find on it any sign of a sigh.
It teaches us to stand still with patience,
And one can also feel real calmness in its presence.
One can pass a long time by giving it a little stare,
And by looking at it, one can forget his despair.
The white snow on it gives our eyes a nice view, quite hard to find;
It's also like a symbol of peace in many people's minds.
But still we destroy it for our own greed
And like to endanger the future of our own breed.
It is helping us by keeping balance in the environment,
But we are making it ugly by creating in it a bad dent.
We must protect it and help it rise;
Otherwise, our future generations may need to pay a heavy price.

Real World

I don't want to live in a real world where people are not truthful to believe.

I don't want to live in a real world where people want only revenge and forget to forgive.

I don't want to live in a real world where people have to do so many tasks.

I don't want to live in a real world where to complete those tasks, people have to wear so many masks.

I don't want to live in a real world where people are fighting and there is no brotherhood.

I don't want to live in a real world where there is war and many children have no childhood.

I don't want to live in a real world where there is no place for honesty.

I don't want to live in a real world where in corruption, people found a new ecstasy.

I don't want to live in a real world where one God has more than one name.

I don't want to live in a real world where people are killing each other for their own God's fame.

I don't want to live in a real world where money is everything.

I don't want to live in a real world where sacrifice and true love have no meaning.

I want to live in a world where nobody can find this world's ugliness;

I want to live in a world where everyone will be happy without any selfishness.

Poverty

Poverty is nothing but a division of the world into two parts for the human being;

Excesses of one part here left the other part with very few things for living.

Poverty is nothing but some people's evil creation,

As a result of which everywhere there is discrimination.

Poverty is some people's design to bring inequality within all of mankind

So that free spirits among society they are easily able to grind.

Poverty is nothing but a very pathetic vicious circle;

That circle is created so that certain people can run their evil cartel.

Poverty is preventing an entire nation from progress,

As a result of which everywhere one can find only distress.

Poverty is preventing certain people from getting a proper education,

Due to which there is no growth in a nation.

Poverty is something which is taking everybody quite a ways backward,

As a result of which many people's minds are filled up with certain dirt.

Poverty is the devil which, at any cost, people need to eradicate

So all people can live happily and are able to write their own fate.

War

Battles were once fought so that justice could become fair.

But today a war is created to fulfill some people's evil desire.

Everywhere, some devils are spreading only false propaganda

So they can fulfill their own evil agenda.

Many places became laboratories to display the power of some freaks,

Human beings living there converted to innocent guinea pigs.

Some demons are saying this war is to save people from terrorism,

But actually it is only to start a new form of imperialism.

Fanatics are trained to have their own free run

So some monsters can raise money for their own fun.

To live in peace silently, you need to follow some fiends' every instruction;

The moment you raise your voice, you will get nothing but destruction.

It's time for us to stop this war and fight for our true freedom;

Otherwise, this world will become a dark place without any wisdom.

A True Friend

A true friend is someone quite difficult to find;

A true friend is someone who gives you complete peace of mind.

A true friend is someone whom you can feel in your heart;

A true friend is someone on whom you will never find any dirt.

A true friend is someone with whom everything you can share;

A true friend is someone who can never be with you unfair.

A true friend is someone who can sometimes be with you naughty;

A true friend is someone with whom you can always feel happy.

A true friend is someone who can understand your every feeling;

A true friend is someone who can for you become, anytime, daring.

A true friend is someone who can never act with you like a fake;

A true friend is someone who can never for you can believe in give-and-take.

A true friend is someone with whom you can always feel secure;

A true friend is someone in whom one can find for you any cure.

A true friend is someone who can do anything for you which you can't expect;

A true friend is someone whom, in your whole life, you will never be able to forget.

Broken World

The world is broken up with so many divisions;

It's due to the formation of so many races, castes, creeds, and religions.

We, all humans, used to call ourselves so civilized,

But our minds have become so marginalized.

We all are, on one hand, following a certain path with strong determination;

We only, on the other hand, kill each other with a mind full of discrimination.

In the name of our own mad thought, we have become so blind.

Due to that, we only have created so many walls around our own minds.

Are we brave enough to move forward?

Or are we moving back like cowards?

Today, we have got so much technology for us to progress,

But we also have got hearts having nothing except distress.

Instead of hating, why can't we love each other?

Why can't we see everyone as our own brother?

Today, my thoughts may sound to many quite strange,

But I am sure one day, this broken world will change.

Printed in the United States
By Bookmasters